HARTFORD PUBLIC LIBRARY
CAMPFIELD BRANCH
30 CAMPFIELD AVENUE
HARTFORD, CT 06114
695-7440

09-AHT-738

WITHDRAWN
Hartford
Public Library
A place like no other.

DK READERS

Level 2

Dinosaur Dinners
Fire Fighter!
Bugs! Bugs! Bugs!
Slinky, Scaly Snakes!
Animal Hospital
The Little Ballerina
Munching, Crunching, Sniffing, and Snooping
The Secret Life of Trees
Winking, Blinking, Wiggling, and Waggling
Astronaut: Living in Space
Twisters!
Holiday! Celebration Days around the World
The Story of Pocahontas
Horse Show
Survivors: The Night the Titanic Sank
Eruption! The Story of Volcanoes
The Story of Columbus
Journey of a Humpback Whale
Amazing Buildings
Feathers, Flippers, and Feet
Outback Adventure: Australian Vacation
Sniffles, Sneezes, Hiccups, and Coughs
Ice Skating Stars
Let's Go Riding
I Want to Be a Gymnast
Starry Sky
Earth Smart: How to Take Care of
    the Environment
Water Everywhere
Telling Time

A Trip to the Theater
Journey of a Pioneer
Inauguration Day
Emperor Penguins
The Great Migration
Star Wars: Journey Through Space
Star Wars: A Queen's Diary
Star Wars: R2-D2 and Friends
Star Wars: Join the Rebels
Star Wars: Clone Troopers in Action
Star Wars: The Adventures of Han Solo
Star Wars: Bounty Hunters for Hire
Star Wars The Clone Wars: Jedi in Training
Star Wars The Clone Wars: Anakin in Action!
Star Wars The Clone Wars: Stand Aside—Bounty
    Hunters!
Star Wars The Clone Wars: Boba Fett: Jedi Hunter
WWE: John Cena
Pokémon: Meet the Pokémon
Pokémon: Meet Ash!
LEGO® Kingdoms: Defend the Castle
LEGO® Friends: Let's Go Riding
LEGO® DC Super Heroes: Super-Villains
LEGO® Legends of Chima™: Tribes of Chima
Meet the X-Men
Indiana Jones: Traps and Snares
¡Insectos! en español
¡Bomberos! en español
La Historia de Pocahontas en español

Level 3

Shark Attack!
Beastly Tales
Titanic
Invaders from Outer Space
Movie Magic
Time Traveler
Bermuda Triangle
Tiger Tales
Plants Bite Back!
Zeppelin: The Age of the Airship
Spies
Terror on the Amazon
Disasters at Sea
The Story of Anne Frank
Abraham Lincoln: Lawyer, Leader, Legend
George Washington: Soldier, Hero, President
Extreme Sports
Spiders' Secrets
The Big Dinosaur Dig
Space Heroes: Amazing Astronauts
The Story of Chocolate
School Days Around the World
Polar Bear Alert!
Welcome to China
My First Ballet Show
Ape Adventures
Greek Myths
Amazing Animal Journeys
Spacebusters: The Race to the Moon
Ant Antics

WWE: Triple H
WWE: Undertaker
Star Wars: Star Pilot
Star Wars: I Want to Be a Jedi
Star Wars: The Story of Darth Vader
Star Wars: Yoda in Action
Star Wars: Forces of Darkness
Star Wars: Death Star Battles
Star Wars: Feel the Force!
Star Wars: The Battle for Naboo
Star Wars: Obi-Wan Kenobi Jedi Knight
Star Wars: The Legendary Yoda
Star Wars: The Clone Wars: Forces of Darkness
Star Wars The Clone Wars: Yoda in Action!
Star Wars The Clone Wars: Jedi Heroes
Marvel Heroes: Amazing Powers
Marvel Avengers: Avengers Assemble!
Pokémon: Explore with Ash and Dawn
Pokémon: Become a Pokémon Trainer
The Invincible Iron Man: Friends and Enemies
Wolverine: Awesome Powers
Abraham Lincoln: Abogado, Líder, Leyenda en
    español
Al Espacio: La Carrera a la Luna en español
Fantastic Four: The World's Greatest Superteam
Indiana Jones: Great Escapes
LEGO® Hero Factory: Heroes in Action
LEGO® Friends: Friends Forever
LEGO® Friends: Summer Adventures
LEGO® Legends of Chima™: The Race for CHI

A Note to Parents

DK READERS is a compelling program for beginning readers, designed in conjunction with leading literacy experts, including Dr. Linda Gambrell, Distinguished Professor of Education at Clemson University. Dr. Gambrell has served as President of the National Reading Conference, the College Reading Association, and the International Reading Association.

Beautiful illustrations and superb full-color photographs combine with engaging, easy-to-read stories to offer a fresh approach to each subject in the series. Each DK READER is guaranteed to capture a child's interest while developing his or her reading skills, general knowledge, and love of reading.

The five levels of DK READERS are aimed at different reading abilities, enabling you to choose the books that are exactly right for your child:

Pre-level 1: Learning to read
Level 1: Beginning to read
Level 2: Beginning to read alone
Level 3: Reading alone
Level 4: Proficient readers

The "normal" age at which a child begins to read can be anywhere from three to eight years old. Adult participation through the lower levels is very helpful for providing encouragement, discussing storylines, and sounding out unfamiliar words.

No matter which level you select, you can be sure that you are helping your child learn to read, then read to learn!

3 2520 10571 1583

LONDON, NEW YORK, MUNICH,
MELBOURNE, and DELHI

Editorial Assistant Ruth Amos
Senior Editor Elizabeth Dowsett
Senior Designer Lynne Moulding
Jacket Designer Lynne Moulding
Pre-production Producer Marc Staples
Producer Charlotte Oliver
Managing Editor Laura Gilbert
Design Manager Maxine Pedliham
Art Director Ron Stobbart
Publishing Director Simon Beecroft

Reading Consultant Dr. Linda Gambrell

Lucasfilm
Executive Editor J. W. Rinzler
Art Director Troy Alders
Keeper of the Holocron Leland Chee
Director of Publishing Carol Roeder

Rovio
Approvals Editor Nita Ukkonen
Senior Graphic Designer Jan Schulte-Tigges
Content Manager Laura Nevanlinna
Vice President of Book Publishing Sanna Lukander

First published in the United States in 2013
by DK Publishing
375 Hudson Street, New York, New York 10014
10 9 8 7 6 5 4 3 2 1

Copyright © 2013 Dorling Kindersley Limited

Angry Birds™ © 2009-2013 Rovio Entertainment Ltd.
All rights reserved.
© 2013 Lucasfilm Ltd. LLC & ® or TM where indicated.
All rights reserved. Used under authorization.

001–193695–June/13

All rights reserved under International and Pan-American
Copyright Conventions. No part of this publication may be
reproduced, stored in a retrieval system, or transmitted in any
form or by any means, electronic, mechanical, photocopying,
recording, or otherwise, without the prior written
permission of the copyright owner.
Published in Great Britain by Dorling Kindersley Limited.

DK books are available at special discounts when purchased in bulk
for sales promotions, premiums, fund-raising, or educational use.
For details, contact:
DK Publishing Special Markets
375 Hudson Street, New York, New York 10014
SpecialSales@dk.com

A catalog record for this book is available
from the Library of Congress.

ISBN: 978-1-4654-0188-5 (Paperback)
ISBN: 978-1-4654-0189-2 (Hardcover)

Color reproduction by Altaimage, UK
Printed and bound in the USA by Lake Book Manufacturing, Inc.

Discover more at
www.dk.com
www.starwars.com

Contents

DK READERS

BEGINNING
2
TO READ ALONE

ANGRY BIRDS STAR WARS

LARD VADER'S VILLAINS

Written by Ruth Amos

The Pork Side

This is a very wicked gang of pigs!
The pigs belong to the Pig Empire and they love to guzzle junk food.

Emperor
Piglatine

Lard Vader

The pigs are trying to find the legendary Egg, which holds the power to rule the galaxy.
First they must defeat the pesky Bird Rebels, who are defending the Bird Republic.
The birds want to be left in peace, but the pigs want power!

Pigtrooper

Boba Fatt

Guard

Lard Vader

Lard Vader is one of the
Pig Empire's chiefs.
His greatest ambition is to find
the mysterious Egg.

A long time ago he was a
Jedi, but then he joined the pigs.
The Jedi are warriors who serve
and protect the Bird Republic.

Lard Vader wants to be the most important pig, so he likes to stand on his Pigtrooper soldiers to seem taller. Unfortunately, he often falls off!

Pigtrooper

Another Pigtrooper!

Emperor Piglatine

Emperor Piglatine is the leader of the Pig Empire. He rules over all the other pigs in the galaxy.

Hidden weapon

The Emperor has banned all delicious junk food and candy in the galaxy, so that he can gobble it all down by himself.

Emperor Piglatine is not a very pretty pig—he has droopy green skin and a slimy snout. Luckily, the rest of his face is covered by a hood!

Lightsabers
The Emperor and his pigs fight with red lightsaber weapons. Bird Rebel warriors use blue ones.

The Emperor's guards

These guards are Emperor Piglatine's personal piggy protection. They are supposed to follow behind the Emperor at all times to protect him.

Shiny visor

Silver forks
These are excellent for shoveling up as much food as possible!

Unfortunately, they are too busy tripping over one another's long robes to protect him!

The guards carry forks to help them deliver junk food and candy to their greedy leader.

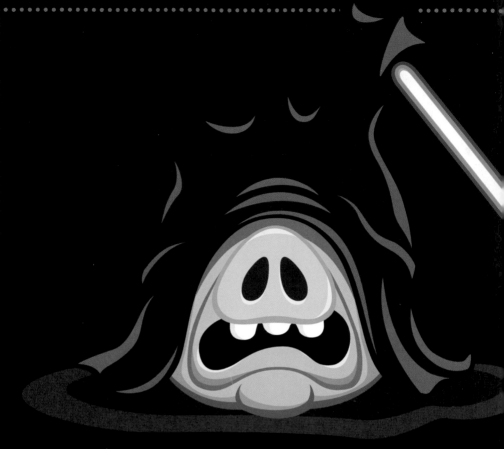

Duel for piggy power

Emperor Piglatine has no idea that Lard Vader wants to be the leader of the pigs. Porky Piglatine is too busy eating as much food as possible to notice.

Button to turn
on lightsaber

Lard Vader often tries
to sneak up on the Emperor
with his lightsaber.
The Emperor thinks it is a
silly joke and just laughs at him!
Vader still hopes to be top pig.

Pigtroopers

Attention! This squadron of Pigtroopers are Emperor Piglatine's soldiers. The Pigtroopers must search the galaxy for junk food and bring it back to the Emperor.

Triangle-shaped snout

Unfortunately, these soldier swine are utterly useless at their job—they often get lost. They hate asking for directions and they are not very good at using their snouts to sniff out clues.

Hard helmet

The Bird Rebels

Squawk! Look who it is!
This fantastic flock is called
the Bird Rebels.
These heroic adventurers must
fight to save the galaxy from the
wicked pigs.

Chuck "Ham" Solo

Terebacca

Red Skywalker

Brilliant blaster
Ham keeps his
blaster weapon in its
holster at his side.

Lard Vader and his villainous
friends keep trying to defeat the
birds, but they are too brave
and clever!

C-3PYOLK

R2-EGG2

Princess
Stella
Organa

Obi-Wan
Kaboomi

Yoda
Bird

The Pig Star

Behold, the Pig Star! The Pig Empire has built an incredible new super weapon, which has the power to blow up the entire universe! The Pig Star has big ears and a round snout, just like the pigs.

The Bird Rebels are terrified
by the Pig Star's ferocious face—
even Princess Stella.

Jabba and bounty hunters

Monstrous Jabba the Hog is a wicked crime lord who secretly sells junk food. He often buys candy from the food smuggler and Bird Rebel, Ham Solo.

Jabba the Hog

Slug-like tail

Jabba likes to work with
other sneaky crooks.
He pays bounty hunter pigs to
track down birds who have escaped,
in exchange for a big sack of treats.
This bounty hunter has bulging
eyes for spotting runaway birds!

Bounty
hunter

Boba Fatt

Boba Fatt is another bounty hunter. Lard Vader pays Boba to zoom around the galaxy on his jetpack and find the *Mighty Falcon*.

Antenna for receiving messages

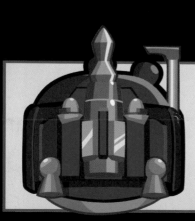

Jetpack
Boba's bright blue-and-orange jetpack propels him through space on his missions.

The *Falcon* is Ham Solo's fantastic starship.

Ham gives the Bird Rebels a ride in it when they go on quests.

Boba tries to stop the *Falcon*.

He wants to take the birds back to Lard Vader, who will give him lots of candy to slurp!

Imperial army

Lard Vader has different kinds of pigs to fight for the Empire. The pigs in white helmets are called Snowtroopers, and they wear special masks to shield their snouts from the cold.

Pig Pilot

Pig Empire symbol

The Pig Pilots who wear black armor are in charge of zooming around the galaxy in aircraft. The Pig Commanders in white have red Pig Empire symbols on their helmets, and they give out silly orders to the Pigtroopers.

The Egg

This is The Egg that Lard Vader and his villains want! The Egg contains the Force— a form of energy that has the power to rule the universe. Yoda Bird disguised The Egg as the bird droid, R2-EGG2, to keep it safe.

Yoda Bird, Red Skywalker,
and Obi-Wan Kaboomi are Jedi
warriors, who study the Force
to defend the Bird Republic.
Red and Obi-Wan use the Force
to try to find The Egg.
Unfortunately, old Yoda Bird
keeps forgetting to tell the
other Jedi where he hid it!

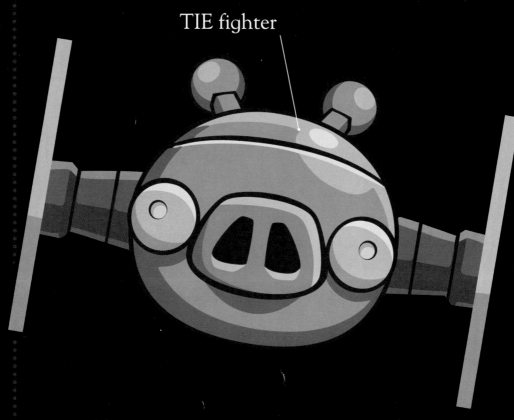

TIE fighter

Villainous vehicles

The wicked Pig Pilots have
plenty of vehicles they use to
carry out their pig patrols.
The pigs fly TIE fighter aircraft
with bulging eyes and big grins.

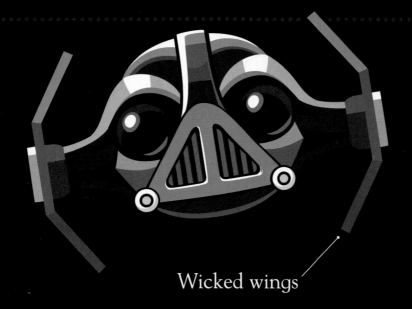

Wicked wings

Lard Vader has his own
fast, personalized TIE fighter
with glowing red eyes.
He expects all the other
TIE fighters to move out
of the way for him!

Breathing tubes
The Pig Pilots' masks
have special breathing
equipment to help
them breathe in space.

Big battle

On the frozen planet of Hoth,
Lard Vader's villains ambush
the Bird Rebels!
The Pig Commanders ride huge
AT-AT walkers across the snow.
Luckily, the Bird Rebels defend
themselves fiercely.

Red strikes with his lightsaber
and Ham Solo fires his blaster.

Victory to the Bird Rebels!
Lard Vader and the Pig Empire
must try again
another day . . .

AT-AT
walker

Quiz

1. Who is the leader of the Pig Empire?

2. What is the name of this vehicle?

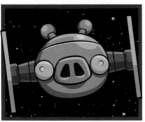

3. Whose side is Red Skywalker on?

4. What is this super weapon called?

5. Where is The Egg hidden?

1. Emperor Piglatine, 2. TIE fighter, 3. Bird Rebels, 4. Pig Star, 5. It is disguised as R2-EGG2